HISTORY'S MOST INFLUENTIAL WRITERS

FROM THE 1600s TO THE 1700s

Miguel de Cervantes to Robert Burns

EDITED BY J.E. LUEBERING

I0801469

Britannica® Educational Publishing

IN ASSOCIATION WITH

ROSEN EDUCATIONAL SERVICES

Published in 2025 by Britannica Educational Publishing
(a trademark of Encyclopædia Britannica, Inc.)
in association with Rosen Educational Services, LLC
2544 Clinton Street, Buffalo, NY 14224.

Copyright © 2025 Encyclopædia Britannica, Inc. Britannica, Encyclopædia Britannica, and the Thistle logo are registered trademarks of Encyclopædia Britannica, Inc. All rights reserved.

Rosen Educational Services materials copyright © 2025 Rosen Educational Services, LLC. All rights reserved.

Distributed exclusively by Rosen Educational Services.
For a listing of additional Britannica Educational Publishing titles, call toll free (800) 237-9932.

First Edition

Britannica Educational Publishing
Michael I. Levy: Executive Editor
Marilyn L. Barton: Senior Coordinator, Production Control
Steven Bosco: Director, Editorial Technologies
Lisa S. Braucher: Senior Producer and Data Editor
Yvette Charboneau: Senior Copy Editor
Kathy Nakamura: Manager, Media Acquisition
J. E. Luebering: Manager and Senior Editor, Literature

Editor: Greg Roza
Book design: Michael Flynn

Photo credits: Cover, p. 21 https://en.wikipedia.org/wiki/File:Cobbe_portrait_of_Shakespeare.jpg; p. 31 https://commons.wikimedia.org/wiki/File:MILTON_(1695)_p016_PL_1.jpg.

Cataloging-in-Publication Data

Names: Luebering, J.E.
Title: From the 1600s to the 1700s: Miguel de Cervantes to Robert Burns / edited by J.E. Luebering.
Description: New York : Britannica Educational Publishing, in Association with Rosen Educational Services, 2025. | Series: History's most influential writers | Includes glossary and index.
Identifiers: ISBN 9781641901086 (library bound) | ISBN 9781641901079 (pbk) | ISBN 9781641901093 (ebook)
Subjects: LCSH: Authors--17th century--Biography. | Literature, Modern--17th century--Bio-bibliography. | Authorship--History--17th century.
Classification: LCC PN451.F766 2025 | DDC 809'.03 B --dc23

Manufactured in the United States of America

CPSIA Compliance Information: Batch #CSBRIT25. For further information contact Rosen Publishing at 1-800-237-9932.

Find us on

CONTENTS

Introduction

"The most original of authors are not so because they advance what is new, but more because they know how to say something, as if it had never been said before."
—Johann Wolfgang von Goethe (1749–1832)

Open a book—any book. In it you'll find words, of course, but look closely and you'll also find art, crafted, in detail, by a writer proud enough to sign his or her name to the work. In a book, or in any piece of writing, words are joined together at the whim of the author. Sentences are created, paragraphs and stanzas formatted, chapters built, and stories told. In a book or a poem, a play or a short story, everything is there, on the page, for a reason: To show, to tell, to convey a message. Most works of writing, quite simply, are meant for reading. The great ones, however, by the most talented and ingenious authors, are for study. In such works, it's the art one finds within that sets them apart from the rest.

Writers are influenced by the places in which they live and the cultures in which they are steeped. The writers in this volume lived during the 1600s and 1700s. Several individuals included in this volume, such as William Shakespeare, are paradigms of English literature. Others were Europeans who wrote in their native tongues in Spain, Italy, France, and Germany. This book also features the work of Basho, a Japanese poet, and Sor Juana Inés de la Cruz, a Mexican writer of great renown.

As the title of this book indicates, all those featured in this collection are influential writers. Through their work, they reached out to the masses, touched the hearts and souls of millions, and left their mark on the world. But how exactly is influence defined in this case? Perhaps it's the ability of one person, through his or her writing, to change the way the world thinks.

Perhaps a writer's influence is determined by timeless prominence, the ability to remain relevant hundreds of years after initial publication. All of the authors in this book fit that bill. This ability to sway audiences so deeply, and in so many ways, several centuries after the fact is arguably the very definition of influential.

With carefully crafted prose or a verse, a writer can influence individual allegiances, support or defame a political regime, or effect change by shedding light on an untenable situation. When all is said and done, perhaps what makes a writer influential is simply the ability to entertain, to keep readers up at night, turning page after page, just so they can learn what happens next.

The truth is, influence can mean so many things and can be measured in so many ways. Those who read the works of any of the writers profiled in this book may very well discover an experience they've perhaps never had before. They might have their imagination sparked and be transported, however briefly, from the travails of the life they're living. An author's writing might, with its insight, highlight an injustice, leading readers to speak out themselves and demand an equitable resolution. Whatever the case, one can't read a work by authors such as those detailed here without being influenced in some way. That's the power of great writing. And that's the real reason we read.

MIGUEL DE CERVANTES

(b. Sept. 29?, 1547, Alcalá de Henares, Spain—d. April 22, 1616, Madrid)

Miguel de Cervantes was a Spanish novelist, playwright, and poet. Best known as the creator of *Don Quixote* (1605, 1615), he is the most important and celebrated figure in Spanish literature. Cervantes tried his hand in all the major literary genres save the epic. He was a notable short-story writer, and a few of those in his collection of *Novelas exemplares* (1613; *Exemplary Stories*) attain a level close to that of *Don Quixote*, on a miniature scale.

A Life Filled with Adventure

Little is known of Cervantes's early education. The supposition, based on a passage in one of the *Exemplary Stories*, that he studied for a time under the Jesuits, though not unlikely, remains conjectural. Unlike most Spanish writers of his time, including some of humble origin, he apparently did not go to a university. What is certain is that at some stage he became an avid reader of books. His first published poem, on the death of Philip II's young queen, Elizabeth of Valois, appeared in 1569. That same year he left Spain for Italy. By 1570 he had enlisted as a soldier in a Spanish infantry regiment stationed in Naples, then a possession of the Spanish crown. He was there for about a year before he saw active service.

A confrontation between the Turkish fleet and the naval forces of Venice, the papacy, and Spain was inevitable at this time. In mid-September 1571 Cervantes sailed on board the *Marquesa*, part of the large fleet under the command of Don Juan de Austria that engaged the enemy on October 7 in the Gulf of Lepanto near Corinth. The fierce battle ended in a crushing defeat for the Turks that was ultimately to break their control of the Mediterranean.

There are independent accounts of Cervantes's conduct in the action, and they concur in testifying to his personal courage. Though stricken with a fever, he refused to stay below and joined the thick of the fighting. He received two gunshot wounds in the chest, and a third rendered his left hand useless for the rest of his life. He always looked back on his conduct in the battle with pride. He set sail for Spain in September 1575 with letters of commendation to the king from the duque de Sessa and Don Juan himself.

On this voyage his ship was attacked and captured by Barbary corsairs. Cervantes, together with his brother Rodrigo, was sold into slavery in Algiers, the center of the Christian slave traffic in the Muslim world. The letters he carried magnified his importance in the eyes of his captors. This had the effect of raising his ransom price, and thus prolonging his captivity, while also, it appears, protecting him from punishment by death, mutilation, or torture when his four daring bids to escape were frustrated. His masters, the renegade Dali Mami and later Hasan Paşa, treated him with considerable leniency in the circumstances, whatever the reason. In September 1580, three years after Rodrigo had earned his freedom, Miguel's family, with the aid and intervention of the Trinitarian friars, raised the 500 gold escudos demanded for his release.

Back in Spain, Cervantes spent most of the rest of his life in a manner that contrasted entirely with his decade of action and danger. He would be constantly short of money and in tedious and exacting employment; it would be 25 years before he scored a major literary success with *Don Quixote*. His first published fiction, *La Galatea* (*Galatea: A Pastoral Romance*), in the newly fashionable genre of the pastoral romance, appeared in 1585. The publisher, Blas de Robles, paid him 1,336 reales for it, a good price for a first book. Cervantes also turned his hand to the writing of drama at this time, the early dawn of the Golden Age of the Spanish theater. He contracted to write two plays for the theatrical manager Gaspar de Porras in 1585, one of which, *La confusa* ("Confusion"), he later described as the best he ever wrote. Many years afterward he claimed to have written 20 or 30 plays in this period, which, he noted, were received by the public without being booed off the stage or having the actors pelted with vegetables. The number is vague. Only two plays certainly survive from this time, the historical tragedy of *La Numancia* (1580s; *Numantia: A Tragedy*) and *El trato de Argel* (1580s; "The Traffic of Algiers").

Though destined to be a disappointed dramatist, Cervantes went on trying to get managers to accept his stage works. By 1587 it was clear that he was not going to make a living from literature, and he was obliged to turn in a very different direction. A series of positions as a civil servant followed. He spent time in jail several times because accounts he oversaw showed discrepancies. After 1598, information about Cervantes's life over the next four or five years is sparse.

Don Quixote

In July or August 1604, Cervantes sold the rights of *El ingenioso hidalgo don Quijote de la Mancha* ("The Ingenious Hidalgo Don Quixote of La Mancha," known as *Don Quixote*, Part I) to the publisher-bookseller Francisco de Robles for an unknown sum. License to publish was granted in September, and the book came out in January 1605. There is some evidence of its content's being known or known about before publication—to, among others, Lope de Vega, the vicissitudes of whose relations with Cervantes were then at a low point. The compositors at Juan de la Cuesta's press in Madrid are now known to have been responsible for a great many errors in the text, many of which were long attributed to the author.

Cervantes's masterpiece *Don Quixote* has been variously interpreted as a parody of chivalric romances, an epic of heroic idealism, a commentary on the author's alienation, and a critique of Spanish imperialism. While the Romantic tradition downplayed the novel's hilarity by transforming Don Quixote into a tragic hero, readers who view it as a parody accept at face value Cervantes's intention to denounce the popular yet outdated romances of his time. *Don Quixote* certainly pokes fun at the adventures of literary knights-errant, but its plot also addresses the historical realities of 17th-century Spain.

The novel was an immediate success, with multiple editions published across Europe. Thomas Shelton's English translation of the first part appeared in 1612. The name of Cervantes was soon to be as well-known in England, France, and Italy as in Spain. The sale of the publishing rights, however, meant that Cervantes made no more financial profit on Part I of his novel. Nevertheless, relative success, still-unsatisfied ambition, and a tireless urge to experiment with the forms of fiction ensured that, at age 57, with less than a dozen years left to him, Cervantes was just entering the most productive period of his career.

In 1613 the 12 *Exemplary Stories* were published. Cervantes's claim in the prologue to be the first to write original novellas (short stories in the Italian manner) in Castilian is substantially justified. Their precise dates of composition are in most cases uncertain. There is some variety in the collection, within the two general categories of romance-based stories and realistic ones. *El coloquio de los perros* ("Colloquy of the Dogs," English translation in *Three Exemplary Novels*, 1952), a quasi-picaresque novella, with its frame tale *El casamiento engañoso* ("The Deceitful Marriage"), is probably Cervantes's most profound and original creation next to *Don Quixote*.

In 1614 Cervantes published *Viage del Parnaso*, a long allegorical poem in a mock-mythological and satirical vein, with a postscript in prose. Having lost all hope of seeing any more of his plays staged, he had eight of them published in 1615, together with eight short comic interludes, in *Ocho comedias, y ocho entremeses nuevos*.

It is not certain when Cervantes began writing Part II, *Segunda parte del ingenioso caballero don Quijote de la Mancha* ("Second Part of the Ingenious Knight Don Quixote of La Mancha"), but he had probably not gotten much more than halfway through by late July 1614. *Don Quixote*, Part II, emerged from the same press as its predecessor late in 1615. It was quickly reprinted outside of Spain. The second part capitalizes on the potential of the first, developing and diversifying without sacrificing familiarity.

Later Years

In his last years Cervantes mentioned several works that apparently did not get as far as the printing press, if indeed he ever actually started writing them. There was *Bernardo* (the name of a legendary Spanish epic hero), the *Semanas del jardín* ("Weeks in the Garden"; a collection of tales, perhaps like Boccaccio's *Decameron*), and the continuation to his *Galatea*. The one that was published, posthumously in 1617, was his last romance, *Los trabaios de Persiles y Sigismunda, historia setentrional* ("The Labors of Persiles and Sigismunda: A Northern Story"). In it Cervantes sought to renovate the heroic romance of adventure and love in the manner of the *Aethiopica* of Heliodorus. It was an intellectually prestigious genre destined to be very successful in 17th-century France. Intended both to edify and to entertain, the *Persiles* is an ambitious work that exploits the mythic and symbolic potential of romance. It was very successful when it appeared.

In the dedication, written three days before he died, Cervantes, "with a foot already in the stirrup," movingly bade farewell to the world. He died in 1616 and was buried in the convent of the Discalced Trinitarians in the Calle de Cantarranas (now the Calle de Lope de Vega). The exact spot is not marked.

LOPE DE VEGA

(b. Nov. 25, 1562, Madrid, Spain—d. Aug. 27, 1635, Madrid)

Lope de Vega was the outstanding dramatist of the Spanish Golden Age, author of as many as 1,800 plays and several hundred shorter dramatic pieces, of which 431 plays and 50 shorter pieces are extant. He acquired a humanistic education from his abundant though haphazard readings in erudite anthologies. In 1583 he took part in the Spanish expedition against the Azores. By this time he had established himself as a playwright in Madrid and was living from his comedias (tragicomic social dramas). He also exercised an undefined role as gentleman attendant or secretary to various nobles, adapting his role as servant or panderer according to the situation. By 1608, however, when Vega was named to a sinecure position as a familiar of the Inquisition and then prosecutor (*promotor fiscal*) of the Apostolic Chamber, he had become a famous poet and was already regarded as the "phoenix of Spanish wits."

After experiencing a deep religious crisis, he entered the first of several religious orders in 1609. From this time on he wrote almost exclusively religious works, though he also continued his theatrical work, which was financially indispensable. In 1614 he entered the priesthood, but his continued service as secretary and panderer hindered him from obtaining the ecclesiastical benefits he sought. New and scandalous romantic relationships eventually followed, in continuation of a pattern Vega pursued throughout his life. In 1627 his verse epic on the life and execution of Mary, Queen of Scots, which was dedicated to Pope Urban VIII, brought in reward a doctorate in theology of the Collegium Sapientiae and the cross of the Order of Malta, out of which came his proud use of the title *Frey* ("Brother"). His closing years were full of gloom, however, and his death in Madrid evoked national mourning.

Vega became identified as a playwright with the comedia, a comprehensive term for the new drama of Spain's Golden Age. Vega's productivity for the stage, however exaggerated by report, remains phenomenal. He claimed to have written an average of 20 sheets a day throughout his life and left untouched scarcely a vein of writing then current. Cervantes called him "the prodigy of nature."

The earliest firm date for a play written by Vega is 1593. By the beginning of the 16th century, through sheer force of creative genius and fertility of invention, Vega had given the comedia its basic formula and raised it to a peak of splendor. It was essentially a social drama, ringing a thousand changes on the accepted foundations of society: respect for crown, for church, and for the human personality, the latter being symbolized in the "point of honor" (*pundonor*) that Vega commended as the best theme of all "since there are none but are strongly moved thereby." This "point of honor" was a matter largely of convention, "honor" being equivalent, in a very limited and brittle sense, to social reputation. It followed that this was a drama less of character than of action and intrigue that rarely, if ever, grasped the true essence of tragedy.

Few of the plays that Vega wrote were perfect, and in theme they range over a vast horizon. But he had an unerring sense for the theme and detail that could move an audience conscious of being on the crest of its country's greatness to respond to a mirroring on the stage of some of the basic ingredients of that greatness. Because of him the comedia became a vast sounding board for every chord in the Spanish consciousness, a "national" drama in the truest sense.

All Vega's plays suffer from haste of composition, partly a consequence of the public's insatiable desire for novelty. His first acts are commonly his best, with the third a hasty cutting of knots or tying up of loose ends that takes scant account both of probability and of psychology. There was, too, a limit to his inventiveness in the recurrence of basic themes and situations, particularly in his cloak and sword plays. But Vega's defects, like his strength, derive from the accuracy with which he projected onto the stage the essence of his country and age. Vega's plays remain true to the great age of Spain into which he had been born and which he had come to know, intuitively rather than by study, as no one had ever known it before.

Vega's nondramatic works in verse and prose filled 21 volumes in 1776–79. Much of this vast output has withered, but its variety remains impressive. Vega wrote pastoral romances, verse histories of recent events, verse biographies of Spanish saints, long epic poems and burlesques upon such works, and prose tales, imitating or adapting works by Ariosto and Cervantes in the process. His lyric compositions—ballads, elegies, epistles, sonnets (there are 1,587 of these)—are myriad. Formally they rely much on the conceit, and in content they provide a running commentary on the poet's whole emotional life.

CHRISTOPHER MARLOWE

(baptized Feb. 26, 1564, Canterbury, Kent, Eng.—d. May 30, 1593, Deptford, near London)

The Elizabethan poet Christopher Marlowe was Shakespeare's most important predecessor in English drama. He is noted especially for his establishment of dramatic blank verse.

Marlowe obtained his Bachelor of Arts degree from the University of Cambridge in 1584. After 1587 he was in London, writing for the theaters, occasionally getting into trouble with the authorities because of his violent and disreputable behavior, and probably also engaging himself from time to time in the government's secret service. Marlowe won a dangerous reputation for "atheism," but this could, in Queen Elizabeth I's time, indicate merely unorthodox religious opinions. There is evidence of his unorthodoxy, notably in the denunciation of him written by the spy Richard Baines and in the letter of the playwright Thomas Kyd to the lord keeper in 1593 after Marlowe's death. Kyd alleged that certain papers "denying the deity of Jesus Christ" that were found in his room belonged to Marlowe, who had shared the room two years before. Whatever the case may be, on May 18, 1593, the Privy Council issued an order for Marlowe's arrest. On May 30, however, he was killed by Ingram Frizer at a lodging house where they and two other men had spent most of the day and where, it was alleged, a fight broke out between them over the bill.

In a playwriting career that spanned little more than six years, Marlowe's achievements were diverse and splendid. Perhaps before leaving Cambridge he had already written *Tamburlaine the Great* (in two parts, both performed by the end of 1587; published 1590), in which he established blank verse as the staple medium for later Elizabethan and Jacobean dramatic writing. Almost certainly during his later Cambridge years, Marlowe had translated Ovid's *Amores* (*The Loves*) and the first book of Lucan's *Pharsalia* from the Latin. About this time he also wrote the play *Dido, Queen of Carthage* (published in 1594 as the joint work of Marlowe and Thomas Nashe). With the production of *Tamburlaine* he received recognition and acclaim, and playwriting became his major concern in the few years that lay ahead. Both parts of *Tamburlaine* were published anonymously in 1590, and the publisher omitted certain passages that he found incongruous with the play's serious concern with history; even so, the extant *Tamburlaine* text can be regarded as substantially Marlowe's. No other of his plays or poems or translations was published during his life. His unfinished but splendid poem *Hero and Leander*, which is almost certainly the finest nondramatic Elizabethan poem apart from those produced by Edmund Spenser, appeared in 1598.

There is argument among scholars concerning the order in which the plays subsequent to *Tamburlaine* were written. It is not uncommonly held that *Faustus* — Marlowe's most famous play, in which he tells the story of the doctor-turned-necromancer Faustus, who sells his soul to the devil in exchange for knowledge and power— quickly followed *Tamburlaine* and that then Marlowe turned to a more neutral, more "social" kind of writing in *Edward II* and *The Massacre at Paris*. His last play may have been *The Jew of Malta*, in which he signally broke new ground: the main character, Barabas, is more closely incorporated within his society than either Tamburlaine, the supreme conqueror, or Faustus, the lonely adventurer against God. It is known that *Tamburlaine, Faustus*, and *The Jew of Malta* were performed by the Admiral's Men, a company whose outstanding actor was Edward Alleyn, who most certainly played Tamburlaine, Faustus, and Barabas the Jew.

WILLIAM SHAKESPEARE

(baptized April 26, 1564, Stratford-upon-Avon, Warwickshire, Eng.—d. April 23, 1616, Stratford-upon-Avon)

William Shakespeare is often called the English national poet and is considered by many to be the greatest dramatist of all time. He occupies a position unique in world literature. Other poets, such as Homer and Dante, and novelists, such as Leo Tolstoy and Charles Dickens, have transcended national barriers as well. But no writer's living reputation can compare to that of Shakespeare, whose plays, written in the late 16th and early 17th centuries for a small repertory theater, are now performed and read more often and in more countries than ever before. The prophecy of his great contemporary, the poet and dramatist Ben Jonson, that Shakespeare "was not of an age, but for all time," has been fulfilled.

Early Life in Stratford

The parish register of Holy Trinity Church in Stratford-upon-Avon, Warwickshire, shows that he was baptized there on April 26, 1564; his birthday is traditionally celebrated on April 23. His father, John Shakespeare, was a burgess of the borough, who in 1565 was chosen an alderman and in 1568 bailiff (the position corresponding to mayor, before the grant of a further charter to Stratford in 1664). He was engaged in various kinds of trade and appears to have suffered some fluctuations in prosperity. His wife, Mary Arden, of Wilmcote, Warwickshire, came from an ancient family and was the heiress to some land.

(Given the somewhat rigid social distinctions of the 16th century, this marriage must have been a step up the social scale for John Shakespeare.)

Stratford enjoyed a grammar school of good quality, and the education there was free, the schoolmaster's salary being paid by the borough. No lists of the pupils who were at the school in the 16th century have survived, but it would be absurd to suppose the bailiff of the town did not send his son there. The boy's education would consist mostly of Latin studies—learning to read, write, and speak the language fairly well and studying some of the Classical historians, moralists, and poets. Shakespeare did not go on to the university, and indeed, it is unlikely that the scholarly round of logic, rhetoric, and other studies then followed there would have interested him.

Instead, at age 18, he married. Where and exactly when are not known, but the episcopal registry at Worcester preserves a bond dated November 28, 1582, and executed by two yeomen of Stratford, named Sandells and Richardson, as a security to the bishop for the issue of a license for the marriage of William Shakespeare and "Anne Hathaway of Stratford," upon the consent of her friends and upon once asking of the banns. (Anne died in 1623, seven years after Shakespeare. There is good evidence to associate her with a family of Hathaways who inhabited a beautiful farmhouse, now much visited, 2 miles [3.2 km] from Stratford.) The next date of interest is found in the records of the Stratford church, where a daughter, named Susanna, born to William Shakespeare, was baptized on May 26, 1583. On February 2, 1585, twins were baptized, Hamnet and Judith. (Hamnet, Shakespeare's only son, died 11 years later.)

How Shakespeare spent the next eight years or so, until his name begins to appear in London theater records, is not known. There are stories—given currency long after his death—of stealing deer and getting into trouble with a local magnate, Sir Thomas Lucy of Charlecote, near Stratford; of earning his living as a schoolmaster in the country; of going to London and gaining entry to the world of theater by minding the horses of theatergoers. It has also been conjectured that Shakespeare spent some time as a member of a great household and that he was a soldier, perhaps in the Low Countries. In lieu of external evidence, such extrapolations about Shakespeare's life have often been made from the internal "evidence" of his writings. But this method is unsatisfactory. One cannot conclude, for example, from his allusions to the law that Shakespeare was a lawyer, for he was clearly a writer who without difficulty could get whatever knowledge he needed for the composition of his plays.

Career in the Theater

The first reference to Shakespeare in the literary world of London comes in 1592, when a fellow dramatist, Robert Greene, declared in a pamphlet written on his deathbed:

> *There is an upstart crow, beautified with our feathers, that with his* Tygers heart wrapt in a Players hide *supposes he is as well able to bombast out a blank verse as the best of you; and, being an absolute* Johannes Factotum, *is in his own conceit the only Shake-scene in a country.*

What these words mean is difficult to determine, but clearly they are insulting, and clearly Shakespeare is the object of the sarcasms. When the book in which they appear (*Greenes, groats-worth of witte, bought with a million of Repentance*, 1592) was published after Greene's death, a mutual acquaintance wrote a preface offering an apology to Shakespeare and testifying to his worth. This preface also indicates that Shakespeare was by then making important friends. For, although the puritanical city of London was generally hostile to the theater, many of the nobility were good patrons of the drama and friends of the actors. Shakespeare seems to have attracted the attention of the young Henry Wriothesley, the 3rd earl of Southampton, and to this nobleman were dedicated his first published poems, *Venus and Adonis* and *The Rape of Lucrece*.

One striking piece of evidence that Shakespeare began to prosper early and tried to retrieve the family's fortunes and establish its gentility is the fact that a coat of arms was granted to John Shakespeare in 1596. Rough drafts of this grant have been preserved in the College of Arms, London, though the final document, which must have been handed to the Shakespeares, has not survived. Almost certainly William himself took the initiative and paid the fees. The coat of arms appears on Shakespeare's monument (constructed before 1623) in the Stratford church. Equally interesting as evidence of Shakespeare's worldly success was his purchase in 1597 of New Place, a large house in Stratford, which he as a boy must have passed every day in walking to school.

How his career in the theater began is unclear, but from roughly 1594 onward he was an important member of the Lord Chamberlain's company of players (called the King's Men after the accession of James I in 1603). They had the best actor, Richard Burbage. They had the best theater, the Globe (finished by the autumn of 1599). They had the best dramatist, Shakespeare. It is no wonder that the company prospered. Shakespeare became a full-time professional man of his own theater, sharing in a cooperative enterprise and intimately concerned with the financial success of the plays he wrote.

Unfortunately, written records give little indication of the way in which Shakespeare's professional life molded his marvelous artistry. All that can be deduced is that for 20 years Shakespeare devoted himself assiduously to his art, writing more than a million words of poetic drama of the highest quality.

Private Life

Shakespeare had little contact with officialdom, apart from walking—dressed in the royal livery as a member of the King's Men—at the coronation of King James I in 1604. He continued to look after his financial interests. He bought properties in London and in Stratford. In 1605 he purchased a share (about one-fifth) of the Stratford tithes—a fact that explains why he was eventually buried in the chancel of its parish church. For some time he lodged with a French Huguenot family called Mountjoy, who lived near St. Olave's Church in Cripplegate, London. The records of a lawsuit in May 1612, resulting from a Mountjoy family quarrel, show Shakespeare as giving evidence in a genial way (though unable to remember certain important facts that would have decided the case) and as interesting himself generally in the family's affairs.

No letters written by Shakespeare have survived, but a private letter to him happened to get caught up with some official transactions of the town of Stratford and so has been preserved in the borough archives. It was written by one Richard Quiney and addressed by him from the Bell Inn in Carter Lane, London, whither he had gone from Stratford on business. On one side of the paper is inscribed: "To my loving good friend and countryman, Mr. Wm. Shakespeare, deliver these." Apparently Quiney thought his fellow Stratfordian a person to whom he could apply for the loan of £30—a large sum in Elizabethan times. Nothing further is known about the transaction, but, because so few opportunities of seeing into Shakespeare's

This painting, first identified in 2009 as depicting William Shakespeare, is believed to be the only true portrait of him made during his lifetime. Authenticity has been an issue with the famous playwright for years. Many have questioned whether Shakespeare actually wrote all the works credited to him.

private life present themselves, this begging letter becomes a touching document. It is of some interest, moreover, that 18 years later Quiney's son Thomas became the husband of Judith, Shakespeare's second daughter.

Shakespeare's will (made on March 25, 1616) is a long and detailed document. It entailed his quite ample property on the male heirs of his elder daughter, Susanna. (Both his daughters were then married, one to the aforementioned Thomas Quiney and the other to John Hall, a respected physician of Stratford.) As an afterthought, he bequeathed his "second-best bed" to his wife; no one can be certain what this notorious legacy means. The testator's signatures to the will are apparently in a shaky hand. Perhaps Shakespeare was already ill. He died on April 23, 1616. No name was inscribed on his gravestone in the chancel of the parish church of Stratford-upon-Avon. Instead these lines, possibly his own, appeared:

Good friend, for Jesus' sake forbear
To dig the dust enclosed here.
Blest be the man that spares these stones,
And curst be he that moves my bones.

Plays and Poems

Other than *Titus Andronicus* (*c.* 1589–92), Shakespeare did not experiment with formal tragedy in his early years. The young playwright was drawn more quickly into comedy, and with more immediate success. These comedies—such as *The Two Gentlemen of Verona* (*c.* 1590–94) and *The Taming of the Shrew* (*c.* 1590–94)—revel in stories of amorous courtship in which a plucky and admirable young woman (played by a boy actor) is paired off against her male wooer. His early history plays represent a genre with very few precedents; such plays as *Richard III* (*c.* 1592–94) were immediately successful.

In the second half of the 1590s, Shakespeare brought to perfection the genre of romantic comedy that he had helped to invent with such plays as *A Midsummer Night's Dream* (*c.* 1595–96), *Much Ado About Nothing* (*c.* 1598–99), and *As You Like It* (*c.* 1598–1600). More history plays completed his dramatization of 15th-century English history. The two genres are nicely complementary: the one deals with courtship and marriage, while the other examines the career of a young man growing up to be a worthy king. The tragedy *Romeo and Juliet* (*c.* 1594–96) is unique among plays of this middle period: it combines elements of romantic comedy and tragedy, yet the tragic vision is not that of the great tragedies that were to follow.

About 1599–1600 Shakespeare turned with unsparing intensity to the exploration of darker issues such as revenge, sexual jealousy, aging, midlife crisis, and death. He began writing not only his great tragedies but a group of plays that are hard to classify in terms of genre: *All's Well That Ends Well*, *Measure for Measure*, and *Troilus and Cressida*, all of which date from 1599 to 1605. One remarkable aspect about Shakespeare's great tragedies is that they proceed through such a staggering range of human emotions, and especially the emotions that are appropriate to the mature years of the human cycle. *Hamlet* (*c.* 1599–1601) cycles through revenge, despondency, and world-weariness. *Othello* (*c.* 1603–04) centers on sexual jealousy in marriage. *King Lear* (*c.* 1605–06) is about aging, generational conflict, and feelings of ingratitude. *Macbeth* (*c.* 1606–07) explores ambition mad enough to kill a father figure who stands in the way. *Antony and Cleopatra* (*c.* 1606–07) studies the exhilarating but ultimately dismaying phenomenon of midlife crisis. Shakespeare then turned to comedies that are usually called romances or tragicomedies; *The Winter's Tale* (*c.* 1609–11) and *The Tempest* (*c.* 1611) are typical in telling stories of wandering and separation that lead eventually to tearful and joyous reunion. *The Tempest* seems to have been intended as Shakespeare's farewell to the theater, although other plays, likely collaborations, followed.

Shakespeare's poetry dates from his early professional years, about 1592–94, during a pause in his theatrical career when the plague closed down much theatrical activity. *Venus and Adonis* (1593) and *The Rape of Lucrece* (1594) are the only works that Shakespeare seems to have shepherded through the printing process. Both owe a good deal to Ovid. His sonnets are more difficult to date, since they cannot have been written all at one time; most scholars set them within the period 1593–1600. As a narrative, the sonnet sequence tells of strong attachment, of jealousy, of grief at separation, of joy at being together and sharing beautiful experiences. But their order of composition is unknown, and Shakespeare did not oversee their publication; it is also unclear whether the sonnets reflect any circumstances in Shakespeare's personal life.

JOHN DONNE

(b. sometime between Jan. 24 and June 19, 1572, London, Eng.—d. March 31, 1631, London)

John Donne, the leading English poet of the Metaphysical school and dean of St. Paul's Cathedral, London (1621–31), is often considered the greatest love poet in the English language. He is also noted for his religious verse and treatises and for his sermons, which rank among the best of the 17th century.

Life and Career

At age 12 Donne matriculated at the University of Oxford, where he studied for three years, and he then most likely continued his education at the University of Cambridge, though he took no degree from either university because as a Roman Catholic he could not swear the required oath of allegiance to the Protestant queen, Elizabeth. Following his studies Donne probably traveled in Spain and Italy and then returned to London to read law, first at Thavies Inn (1591) and then at Lincoln's Inn (1592–94). In 1596 he took part in expeditions led by the Earl of Essex and Sir Walter Raleigh.

After his return to London in 1597, Donne became secretary to Sir Thomas Egerton, lord keeper of the great seal, in whose employ Donne remained for almost five years. The appointment itself makes it probable that Donne had become an Anglican by this time. Donne met and fell in love with Anne More, niece of Egerton's second wife and the daughter of Sir George More, who was chancellor of the garter. The two married secretly, probably in December 1601. Because of the marriage, all possibilities of a career in public service were dashed, and Donne found himself at age 30 with neither prospects for employment nor adequate funds with which to support his household. During the next 10 years Donne lived in poverty and humiliating dependence, yet he wrote and studied assiduously, producing prose works on theology and canon law and composing love lyrics, religious poetry, and complimentary and funerary verse for his patrons. In 1612 a newfound patron, Sir Robert Drury, provided the Donnes with a house in London.

In 1614 Donne had come to believe he had a religious vocation, and he finally agreed to take holy orders. He was made a royal chaplain and received, at the king's command, the degree of doctor of divinity from Cambridge. Two years after his ordination, in 1617, Anne Donne died after giving birth to a stillborn child. Grief-stricken, Donne vowed never to marry again. His bereavement turned him fully to his vocation as an Anglican divine. In 1621 he was installed as dean of St. Paul's Cathedral. The power and eloquence of Donne's sermons soon secured for him a reputation as the foremost preacher in the England of his day, and he became a favorite of both King James I and King Charles I.

Poetry

Because almost none of Donne's poetry was published during his lifetime, it is difficult to date it accurately. Most of his poems were preserved in manuscript copies made by and passed among a relatively small but admiring coterie of poetry lovers. Donne's *Anniversaries* were published in 1611–12 and were the only important poetic works by him published in his lifetime.

Donne's poetry is marked by strikingly original departures from the conventions of 16th-century English verse, particularly that of Sir Philip Sidney and Edmund Spenser. Even his early satires and elegies, which derive from classical Latin models, contain versions of his experiments with genre, form, and imagery. His poems contain few descriptive passages like those in Spenser, nor do his lines follow the smooth metrics and euphonious sounds of his predecessors. Donne replaced their mellifluous lines with a speaking voice whose vocabulary and syntax reflect the emotional intensity of a confrontation. One consequence of this is a directness of language that electrifies his mature poetry. "For Godsake hold your tongue, and let me love," begins his love poem "The Canonization," plunging the reader into the midst of an encounter between the speaker and an unidentified listener.

From these explosive beginnings, the poems develop as closely reasoned arguments or propositions that rely heavily on the use of the conceit—i.e., an extended metaphor that draws an ingenious parallel between apparently dissimilar situations or objects. Donne, however, transformed the conceit into a vehicle for transmitting multiple, sometimes even contradictory, feelings and ideas. And, changing again the practice of earlier poets, he drew his imagery from such diverse fields as alchemy, astronomy, medicine, politics, global exploration, and philosophical disputation. These conceits offer brilliant and multiple insights into the subject of the metaphor and help give rise to the much-praised ambiguity of Donne's lyrics.

Prose

Donne's earliest prose works, including *Paradoxes and Problems*, probably were begun during his days as a student at Lincoln's Inn. In 1611 Donne completed his *Essays in Divinity*, the first of his theological works. Upon recovering from a life-threatening illness, Donne in 1623 wrote *Devotions upon Emergent Occasions*, the most enduring of his prose works. Each of its 23 devotions consists of a meditation, an expostulation, and a prayer, all occasioned by some event in Donne's illness, such as the arrival of the king's personal physician or the application of pigeons to draw vapors from Donne's head. The *Devotions* correlate Donne's physical decline with spiritual sickness, until both reach a climax when Donne hears the tolling of a passing bell and questions whether the bell is ringing for him. Like Donne's poetry, the *Devotions* are notable for their dramatic immediacy and their numerous Metaphysical conceits, such as the well-known "No man is an *Iland*," by which Donne illustrates the unity of all Christians in the mystical body of Christ.

It is Donne's sermons, however, that most powerfully illustrate his mastery of prose. One-hundred and fifty-six of them were published by his son in three great folio editions (1640, 1649, and 1661). Though composed during a time of religious controversy, Donne's sermons—intellectual, witty, and deeply moving—explore the basic tenets of Christianity rather than engage in theological disputes. The power of his sermons derives from their dramatic intensity, candid personal revelations, poetic rhythms, and striking conceits.

JOHN MILTON

(b. Dec. 9, 1608, London, Eng.—d. Nov. 8?, 1674, London?)

John Milton, an English poet and pamphleteer, is considered the most significant English author after William Shakespeare. Milton is best known for *Paradise Lost*, widely regarded as the greatest epic poem in English. Together with *Paradise Regained* and *Samson Agonistes*, it confirms Milton's reputation as one of the greatest English poets.

Milton enrolled at Christ's College, Cambridge, in 1625. A year later he was "rusticated," or temporarily expelled, for a period of time because of a conflict with one of his tutors. He was later reinstated. In 1629 Milton was awarded a Bachelor of Arts degree, and in 1632 he received a Master of Arts degree. Despite his initial intent to enter the ministry, Milton did not do so, a situation that has not been fully explained. While at Cambridge he wrote poems in Latin, Italian, and English. Among the most important of these are the companion poems *L'Allegro* and *Il Penseroso*, both published later in *Poems*

(1645); Milton's first published poem in English, *On Shakespeare*, composed in 1630 and published anonymously in the Second Folio (1632) of Shakespeare's plays; and *On the Morning of Christ's Nativity*. In 1632–39 he engaged in private study—writing the masque *Comus* (first performed 1634) and the elegy *Lycidas* (1638)—and toured Europe, spending most of his time in Italy. The Florentine academies especially appealed to Milton, and he befriended young members of the Italian literati, whose similar humanistic interests he found gratifying. Invigorated by their admiration for him, he corresponded with his Italian friends after his return to England. While in Florence, Milton also met with Galileo, who was under house arrest.

Having returned from abroad in 1639, Milton turned his attention from poetry to prose. In doing so, he entered the controversies surrounding the abolition of the Church of England and of the Royalist government, at times replying to, and often attacking vehemently, English and Continental polemicists who targeted him as the apologist of radical religious and political dissent. His best-known prose is in the pamphlets *Areopagitica* (1644), on freedom of the press, and *Of Education* (1644). He mounted a cogent, radical argument, informed by the concepts of personal liberty and individual volition, for divorce in four tracts published 1643–45. He also wrote tracts against the Church of England and against the monarchy. Among the antimonarchical polemics of 1649–55 is *The Tenure of Kings and Magistrates* (1649), composed after Milton had become allied to those who sought to form an English republic but probably written before and during the trial of King Charles I though not published until after his death on January 30, 1649; it urges the abolition of tyrannical kingship and the execution of tyrants. Thereafter, Milton was appointed secretary for foreign tongues (also called Latin secretary) for the Council of

State, the executive body of the Commonwealth under Oliver Cromwell. Milton was entrusted with the duties of translating foreign correspondence, drafting replies, composing papers in which national and international affairs of state were addressed, and serving as an apologist for the Commonwealth against attacks from abroad.

He lost his sight about 1651 and thereafter dictated his works. After the Restoration he was arrested as a prominent defender of the Commonwealth but was soon released. His focus returned to poetry. Abandoning an earlier plan to compose an epic on the legendary British king Arthur, Milton instead turned to biblical subject matter and to a Christian idea of heroism. *Paradise Lost*, considered the greatest epic poem in English, was the result. It was first published in 10 books in 1667 and then in 12 books in 1674, at a length of almost 11,000 lines. It uses blank verse and reworks Classical epic conventions to recount the Fall of Man. *Paradise Lost* is ultimately not only about the downfall of Adam and Eve but also about the clash between Satan and the Son. Many readers have admired Satan's splendid recklessness, if not heroism, in confronting the Godhead. Satan's defiance, anger, willfulness, and resourcefulness define a character who strives never to yield. *Paradise Regained* (1671) is a shorter epic in which Christ overcomes Satan the tempter. It unfolds as a series of debates—an ongoing dialectic—in which Jesus analyzes and refutes Satan's arguments. Though *Paradise Regained* lacks the vast scope of *Paradise Lost*, it fulfills its purpose admirably by pursuing the idea of Christian heroism as a state of mind. More so than *Paradise Lost*, it dramatizes the inner workings of the mind of Jesus, his perception, and the interplay of faith and reason in his debates with Satan. Milton's third great long poem, *Samson Agonistes* (1671), is a dramatic poem in which the Old Testament figure conquers self-pity and despair to become God's champion.

Images from John Milton's Paradise Lost *underscore the epic poem's sense of despair and regret. Patterned after the biblical story of Adam and Eve, the work also details Satan's battle with Jesus for immortal souls.*

Among prose works published late in Milton's life or after his death are *History of Britain*, which was incomplete when published in 1670, and an unfinished work on theology, which was discovered in 1832. The exact date and location of Milton's death remain unknown; he likely died from complications of the gout (possibly renal failure). He was buried inside St. Giles Cripplegate Church in London.

JEAN RACINE

(baptized Dec. 22, 1639, La Ferté-Milon, France—d. April 21, 1699, Paris)

Jean Racine was a dramatic poet and historiographer renowned for his mastery of French classical tragedy. He was not only a contemporary of Molière, the father of modern French comedy, but his career intersected with that of the man who rivalled him for the title of the greatest of all French playwrights.

Orphaned at an early age, Racine was educated in a Jansenist convent, and he chose drama in defiance of his upbringing. His first play, *Amasie*, was never produced and has not survived. His career as a dramatist began with the production by Molière's troupe of his play *La Thébaïde ou les frères ennemis* ("The Thebaide or the Enemy Brothers") at the Palais-Royal Theater in 1664. Molière's troupe also produced Racine's next play, *Alexandre le grand* (*Alexander the Great*), which premiered at the Palais Royal in 1665. This play was so well received that Racine secretly negotiated with the Hôtel de Bourgogne, a rival troupe, to present a "second premiere" of *Alexandre*. The break with Molière was irrevocable; Racine even seduced Molière's leading actress, Thérèse du Parc, into joining him personally and professionally.

Molière hardly slackened his theatrical activity, however. Born Jean-Baptiste Poquelin in 1622 to a prosperous upholsterer, Molière had left home to become an actor in 1643, joining forces with the Béjart family. He cofounded the troupe known as the Illustre Théâtre and toured the French provinces (1645–58), writing plays and acting in them. After his troupe was established in a permanent theater in Paris under the patronage of Louis XIV, he won acclaim in the court and among bourgeois audiences for his comedy *Les Précieuses ridicules* (1659; *The Affected Young Ladies*). His other major plays include *L'École des femmes* (1662; *The School for Wives*), *Tartuffe* (1664; initially banned by religious authorities), *Le Misanthrope* (1666), and *Le Malade imaginaire* (1673; *The Imaginary Invalid*), among others. His plays represent a portrait of all levels of 17th-century French society and are marked by their good-humored and intelligent mockery of human vices, vanities, and follies. Taken ill during a performance in February 1673, he died of a hemorrhage within a day. As he had not been given the sacraments or the opportunity of formally renouncing the actor's profession, he was buried without ceremony.

Racine, after having made off with Thérèse du Parc in 1665, saw her star in his successful *Andromaque* (1667), which explored his theme of the tragic folly of passionate love. The three-act comedy *Les Plaideurs* (1668; *The Litigants*) offered Racine the opportunity to demonstrate his skill in Molière's privileged domain, as well as the occasion to display his expertise in Greek, of which he had better command than almost any nonprofessional classicist in France. The result, a brilliant satire of the French legal system, was an adaptation of Aristophanes' *The Wasps* that found much more favor at court than on the Parisian stage. The great tragedies *Britannicus* (1669), *Bérénice* (1670), and *Bajazet* (1672) followed. *Bérénice* marked the decisive point in Racine's theatrical career, for with this play he found a felicitous combination of elements that he would use, without radical alteration, for the rest of his secular tragedies: a love interest, a relatively uncomplicated plot, striking rhetorical passages, and a highly poetic use of time.

Phèdre (1677) is Racine's supreme accomplishment because of the rigor and simplicity of its organization, the emotional power of its language, and the profusion of its images and meanings. Racine presents Phaedra as consumed by an incestuous passion for her stepson, Hippolytus. Receiving false information that her husband, King Theseus, is dead, Phaedra declares her love to Hippolytus, who is horrified. Theseus returns and is falsely informed that Hippolytus has been the aggressor toward Phaedra. Theseus invokes the aid of the god Neptune to destroy his son, after which Phaedra kills herself out of guilt and sorrow. A structural pattern of cycles and circles in *Phèdre* reflects a conception of human existence as essentially changeless, recurrent, and therefore asphyxiatingly tragic. The play constitutes a daring representation of the contagion of sin and its catastrophic results. After writing his masterpiece, Racine retired to become official historian to Louis XIV. His final plays, *Esther* (1689) and *Athalie* (1691), were commissioned by the king's wife, Madame de Maintenon. Racine died in 1699 from cancer of the liver.

APHRA BEHN

(b. 1640?, Harbledown?, Kent, Eng.—d. April 16, 1689, London)

Aphra Behn, an English dramatist, fiction writer, and poet, was the first Englishwoman known to earn her living by writing. Her origin remains a mystery, in part because Behn may have deliberately obscured her early life. One tradition identifies Behn as the child known only as Ayfara or Aphra, who traveled in the 1650s with a couple named Amis to Suriname, which was then an English possession. She was more likely the daughter of a barber, Bartholomew Johnson, who may or may not have sailed with her and the rest of her family to Suriname in 1663. She returned to England in 1664 and married a merchant named Behn; he died (or the couple separated) soon after. Her wit and talent having brought her into high esteem, she was employed by King Charles II in secret service in the Netherlands in 1666. Unrewarded and briefly imprisoned for debt, she began to write to support herself.

Behn's early works were tragicomedies in verse. In 1670 her first play, *The Forc'd Marriage*, was produced, and *The Amorous Prince* followed a year later. Her sole tragedy, *Abdelazer*, was staged in 1676. However, she turned increasingly to light comedy and farce over the course of the 1670s. Many of these witty and vivacious comedies, notably *The Rover* (two parts, produced 1677 and 1681), were commercially successful. *The Rover* depicts the adventures of a small group of English Cavaliers in Madrid and Naples during the exile of the future Charles II. *The Emperor of the Moon*, first performed in 1687, presaged the harlequinade, a form of comic theater that evolved into the English pantomime.

Though Behn wrote many plays, her fiction today draws more interest. Her short novel *Oroonoko* (1688) tells the story of an enslaved African prince whom Behn claimed to have known in South America. Its engagement with the themes of slavery, race, and gender, as well as its influence on the development of the English novel, helped to make it, by the turn of the 21st century, her best-known work. Behn's other fiction includes the multipart epistolary novel *Love-Letters Between a Nobleman and His Sister* (1684–87) and *The Fair Jilt* (1688).

Behn's versatility, like her output, was immense; she wrote other popular works of fiction, and she often adapted works by older dramatists. She also wrote poetry, the bulk of which was collected in *Poems upon Several Occasions, with A Voyage to the Island of Love* (1684) and *Lycidus; or, The Lover in Fashion* (1688). Behn's charm and generosity won her a wide circle of friends, and her relative freedom as a professional writer, as well as the subject matter of her works, made her the object of some scandal.

BASHO

(b. 1644, Ueno, Iga province, Japan—d. Nov. 28, 1694, Ōsaka)

Bashō is the supreme Japanese haiku poet. He greatly enriched the 17-syllable haiku form and made it an accepted medium of artistic expression.

Interested in haiku from an early age, Bashō—in full Matsuo Bashō, a pseudonym of Matsuo Munefusa—at first put his literary interests aside and entered the service of a local feudal lord. After his lord's death in 1666, however, Bashō abandoned his samurai (warrior) status to devote himself to poetry. Moving to the capital city of Edo (now Tokyo), he gradually acquired a reputation as a poet and critic. In 1679 he wrote his first verse in the "new style" for which he came to be known:

On a withered branch
A crow has alighted:
Nightfall in autumn.

The simple descriptive mood evoked by this statement and the comparison and contrast of two independent phenomena became the hallmark of Bashō's style. He attempted to go beyond the stale dependence on form and ephemeral allusions to current gossip that had been characteristic of haiku, which in his day had amounted to little but a popular literary pastime. Instead he insisted that the haiku must be at once unhackneyed and eternal. Following the Zen philosophy he studied, Bashō attempted to compress the meaning of the world into the simple pattern of his poetry, disclosing hidden hopes in small things and showing the interdependence of all objects.

In 1684 Bashō made the first of many journeys that figure so importantly in his work. His accounts of his travels are prized not only for the haiku that record various sights along the way but also for the equally beautiful prose passages that furnish the backgrounds. *Oku no hosomichi* (1694; *The Narrow Road to the Deep North*), describing his visit to northern Japan, is one of the loveliest works of Japanese literature.

On his travels Bashō also met local poets and competed with them in composing the linked verse (*renga*), an art in which he so excelled that some critics believe his *renga* were his finest work. When Bashō began writing *renga* the link between successive verses had generally depended on a pun or play on words, but he insisted that poets must go beyond mere verbal dexterity and link their verses by "perfume," "echo," "harmony," and other delicately conceived criteria.

One term frequently used to describe Bashō's poetry is *sabi*, which means the love of the old, the faded, and the unobtrusive, a quality found in the verse

Scent of chrysanthemums . . .
And in Nara
All the ancient Buddhas.

Here the musty smell of the chrysanthemums blends with the visual image of the dusty, flaking statues in the old capital. Living a life that was in true accord with the gentle spirit of his poetry, Bashō maintained an austere, simple hermitage that contrasted with the general flamboyance of his times. On occasion he withdrew from society altogether, retiring to Fukagawa, site of his Bashō-an ("Cottage of the Plantain Tree"), a simple hut from which the poet derived his pen name. Later men, honoring both the man and his poetry, revered him as the saint of the haiku.

The Narrow Road to Oku (1996), Donald Keene's translation of *Oku no hosomichi*, provides the original text and a modern-language version by Kawabata Yasunari. *The Monkey's Straw Raincoat and Other Poetry of the Basho School* (1981), a translation by Earl Miner and Hiroko Odagiri, presents a celebrated linked-verse sequence in which Bashō took part, along with a commentary.

SOR JUANA INÉS DE LA CRUZ

(b. Nov. 12, 1651?, San Miguel Nepantla, Viceroyalty of New Spain [now in Mexico]—d. April 17, 1695, Mexico City)

The poet, dramatist, scholar, and nun who came to be known as Sor Juana Inés de la Cruz was an outstanding writer of the Latin American colonial period and of the Hispanic Baroque.

Juana Ramírez de Asbaje was born out of wedlock to a family of modest means in either 1651 or, according to a baptismal certificate, 1648. Her mother was a Creole and her father Spanish. Juana's mother sent the gifted child to live with relatives in Mexico City. There her prodigious intelligence attracted the attention of the viceroy, Antonio Sebastián de Toledo, marquis de Mancera. He invited her to court as a lady-in-waiting in 1664 and later had her knowledge tested by some 40 noted scholars. In 1667, given what she called her "total disinclination to marriage" and her wish "to have no fixed occupation which might curtail my freedom to study," Sor (Spanish: "Sister") Juana began her life as a nun with a brief stay in the order of the Discalced Carmelites. She moved in 1669 to the more lenient Convent of Santa Paula of the Hieronymite order in Mexico City, and there she took her vows.

Convent life afforded Sor Juana time to study and write and the opportunity to teach music and drama to the girls in Santa Paula's school. She also functioned as the convent's archivist and accountant. In her convent cell, Sor Juana amassed one of the largest private libraries in the New World, together with a collection of musical and scientific instruments. The patronage of the viceroy and vicereine of New Spain, notably that of the marquis and marquise de la Laguna from 1680 to 1688, helped her maintain her exceptional freedom. They visited her, favored her, and had her works published in Spain. For her part, Sor Juana, though cloistered, became the unofficial court poet in the 1680s.

Sor Juana was the last great writer of the Hispanic Baroque and the first great exemplar of colonial Mexican culture. She employed all of the poetic models then in fashion, including sonnets, romances (ballad form), and so on. She drew on a vast stock of Classical, biblical, philosophical, and mythological sources. She wrote moral, satiric, and religious lyrics, along with many poems of praise to court figures. Though it is impossible to date much of her poetry, it is clear that, even after she became a nun, Sor Juana wrote secular love lyrics. She also authored both allegorical religious dramas and entertaining cloak-and-dagger plays. Notable in the popular vein are the *villancicos* (carols) that she composed to be sung in the cathedrals of Mexico City, Puebla, and Oaxaca.

Sor Juana celebrated woman as the seat of reason and knowledge rather than passion. Her poem *Hombres necios*

("Foolish Men") accuses men of the illogical behavior that they criticize in women. Her many love poems in the first person show a woman's *desengaño* ("disillusionment") with love, given the strife, pain, jealousy, and loneliness that it occasions. Sor Juana's most significant full-length plays involve the actions of daring, ingenious women. Sor Juana also occasionally wrote of her native Mexico. The short play that introduces her religious drama *El divino Narciso* (1689; *The Divine Narcissus*, in a bilingual edition) blends the Aztec and Christian religions. Her various carols contain an amusing mix of Nahuatl (a Mexican Indian language) and Hispano-African and Spanish dialects. Sor Juana's most important and most difficult poem, known as the *Primero sueño* (1692; *First Dream*), is both personal and universal. The date of its writing is unknown. It employs the convoluted poetic forms of the Baroque to recount the torturous quest of the soul for knowledge.

Sor Juana achieved considerable renown in Mexico and in Spain. With renown came disapproval from church officials. Sor Juana broke with her Jesuit confessor, Antonio Núñez de Miranda, in the early 1680s because he had publicly maligned her. The nun's privileged situation began definitively to collapse after the departure for Spain of her protectors, the marquis and marquise de la Laguna. In November 1690, Manuel Fernández de Santa Cruz, bishop of Puebla, published without Sor Juana's permission her critique of a 40-year-old sermon by the Portuguese Jesuit preacher António Vieira. Fernández de Santa Cruz titled the critique *Carta atenagórica* ("Letter Worthy of Athena"). Using the female pseudonym of Sister Filotea, he also admonished Sor Juana to concentrate on religious rather than secular studies. Sor Juana responded to the bishop of Puebla in March 1691 with her magnificent self-defense and defense of all women's right to knowledge, the *Respuesta a sor Filotea de la Cruz* ("Reply to Sister Filotea of the Cross"). In the autobiographical section of the document, Sor Juana traces the many obstacles that her powerful "inclination to letters" had forced her to surmount throughout her life.

Yet by 1694 Sor Juana had succumbed in some measure to external or internal pressures. She curtailed her literary pursuits. Her library and collections were sold for alms. She returned to her previous confessor, renewed her religious vows, and signed various penitential documents. Sor Juana died while nursing her sister nuns during an epidemic.

DANIEL DEFOE

(b. 1660, London, Eng.—d. April 24, 1731, London)

Daniel Defoe was an English novelist, pamphleteer, and journalist. He remains best known as the author of *Robinson Crusoe* (1719–22) and *Moll Flanders* (1722).

Although intended for the Presbyterian ministry, Defoe decided against this, and by 1683 had set up as a merchant. He dealt in many commodities, traveled widely at home and abroad, and became an acute and intelligent economic theorist.

In 1692, however, after prospering for a while, Defoe went bankrupt. The main reason for his bankruptcy was the loss that he sustained in insuring ships during the war with France—he was one of 19 "merchants insurers" ruined in 1692. He suffered further severe losses in 1703, when his prosperous brick-and-tile works near Tilbury failed during his imprisonment for political offenses, and he did not actively engage in trade after this time.

With Defoe's interest in trade went an interest in politics, both foreign and domestic. The first of many political pamphlets by him appeared in 1683. He was a supporter of William of Orange—"*William*, the Glorious, Great, and

Good, and Kind," as Defoe was to call him—and Defoe supported him loyally, becoming his leading pamphleteer. In 1701, in reply to attacks on the "foreign" king, Defoe published his vigorous and witty poem *The True-Born Englishman*, an enormously popular work. The most famous and skillful of all his pamphlets, "The Shortest-Way With The Dissenters" (1702), was published anonymously but resulted in his being fined and sentenced to stand three times in the pillory, a prosecution that was likely primarily political, driven by an attempt to force him into betraying certain political allies. Although apprehensive of his punishment, Defoe had spirit enough, while awaiting his ordeal, to write the audacious "Hymn To The Pillory" (1703). This helped to turn the occasion into something of a triumph, with the pillory garlanded, the mob drinking his health, and the poem on sale in the streets.

Perhaps Defoe's most remarkable achievement at this time was his periodical, the *Review*. He wrote this serious, forceful, and long-lived paper practically single-handedly from 1704 to 1713. At first a weekly, it became a thrice-weekly publication in 1705, and Defoe continued to produce it even when, for short periods in 1713, his political enemies managed to have him imprisoned again on various pretexts. It was, effectively, the main government organ. But, in addition to politics as such, Defoe discussed current affairs in general, religion, trade, manners, morals, and so on. His work undoubtedly had a considerable influence on the development of later essay periodicals (such as Richard Steele and Joseph Addison's *The Tatler* and *The Spectator*) and of the newspaper press.

With George I's accession (1714), Defoe continued to write for the government of the day and to carry out intelligence work. At about this time (perhaps prompted by a severe illness), he wrote the most popular of his many didactic works, *The Family Instructor* (1715). His writings to this point in his career would not necessarily have procured literary immortality for Defoe; this he achieved when in 1719 he turned to an extended work of prose fiction and (drawing partly on the memoirs of voyagers and castaways such as Alexander Selkirk) produced *Robinson Crusoe*. A German critic has called it a "world-book," a label justified not only by the enormous number of translations, imitations, and adaptations that have appeared but by the almost mythic power with which Defoe creates a hero and a situation with which every reader can in some sense identify.

Here (as in his works of the remarkable year 1722, which saw the publication of *Moll Flanders*, *A Journal of the Plague Year*, and *Colonel Jack*) Defoe displays his finest gift as a novelist—his insight into human nature. The men and women he writes about are all, it is true, placed in unusual circumstances; they are all, in one sense or another, solitaries; they all struggle, in their different ways, through a life that is a constant scene of jungle warfare; they all become, to some extent, obsessive. They are also ordinary human beings, however, and Defoe, writing always in the first person, enters into their minds and analyzes their motives. His novels are given verisimilitude by their matter-of-fact style and their vivid concreteness of detail; the latter may seem unselective, but it effectively helps to evoke a particular, circumscribed world. Defoe's range is narrow, but within that range he is a novelist of considerable power, and his plain, direct style, as in almost all of his writing, holds the reader's interest.

In 1724 he published his last major work of fiction, *Roxana*, though in the closing years of his life, despite failing health, he remained active and enterprising as a writer. In 1724–26 were published the three volumes of Defoe's animated and informative *Tour Through the Whole Island of*

Great Britain, based in large part on his visits to Scotland, especially at the time of the Act of Union in 1707.

JONATHAN SWIFT

(b. Nov. 30, 1667, Dublin, Ire.—d. Oct. 19, 1745, Dublin)

The Anglo-Irish author Jonathan Swift is among the foremost prose satirists in the English language. Besides the celebrated novel *Gulliver's Travels* (1726), he wrote such shorter works as *A Tale of a Tub* (1704) and *A Modest Proposal* (1729).

In 1682 Swift entered Trinity College, Dublin, where he was granted his Bachelor of Arts degree in 1686 and continued in residence as a candidate for his Master of Arts degree until 1689. But the Roman Catholic disorders that had begun to spread through Dublin after the Glorious Revolution (1688–89) in Protestant England caused Swift, a Protestant, to seek security in England. In 1692 he received the degree of M.A. at the University of Oxford. During a return visit to Ireland, he took orders in the Anglican church, being ordained priest in January 1695.

Between 1691 and 1694 Swift wrote a number of poems, notably six odes. But his true genius did not find expression until he turned from verse to prose satire and composed, between 1696 and 1699, *A Tale of a Tub*. Published anonymously in 1704, this work is outstanding for its exuberance of satiric wit and energy and is marked by an incomparable command of stylistic effects, largely in the nature of parody.

After 1699, Swift returned to Dublin as chaplain and secretary to the earl of Berkeley, who was then going to Ireland as a lord justice. During the ensuing years he was in England on some four occasions—in 1701, 1702, 1703, and 1707 to 1709—and won wide recognition in London for his intelligence and his wit as a writer. Early in 1700 he was preferred to several posts in the Irish church. His public writings of this period show that he kept in close touch with affairs in both Ireland and England. Swift's works brought him to the attention of a circle of Whig writers led by Joseph Addison, but Swift was uneasy about many policies of the Whig administration. He was a Whig by birth, education, and political principle, but he was also passionately loyal to the Anglican church, and he came to view with apprehension the Whigs' growing determination to yield ground to the Nonconformists.

A momentous period began for Swift when, in 1710, he once again found himself in London. A Tory ministry headed by Robert Harley (later earl of Oxford) and Henry St. John (later Viscount Bolingbroke) was replacing that of the Whigs. Swift's reactions to such a rapidly changing world are vividly recorded in his *Journal to Stella*, a series of letters written between his arrival in England in 1710 and 1713. The astute Harley made overtures to Swift and won him over to the Tories. Swift quickly became the Tories' chief pamphleteer and political writer. He was rewarded for his services in April 1713 with his appointment as dean of St. Patrick's Cathedral in Dublin. With the accession of George I, the Tories were a ruined party, and Swift's career in England was at an end. He withdrew to Ireland, where he was to pass most of the remainder of his life.

After a period of seclusion, Swift gradually regained his energy. He turned again to verse, which he continued to write throughout the 1720s and early '30s, producing the impressive poem *Verses on the Death of Doctor Swift*, among others. By 1720 he was also showing a renewed interest in public affairs. In his Irish pamphlets of this period he came to grips with many of the problems, social and economic, then confronting Ireland. Of his Irish writings, *A Modest Proposal* remains perhaps the best known. It is a grimly ironic letter of advice in which a public-spirited citizen suggests that Ireland's overpopulation and dire economic conditions could be alleviated if the babies of poor Irish parents were sold as edible delicacies to be eaten by the rich.

Swift's greatest satire, *Gulliver's Travels*, was published in 1726. It is uncertain when he began this work, but it appears from his correspondence that he was writing in earnest by 1721 and had finished the whole by August 1725. Its success was immediate. This work, which is told in Gulliver's "own words," is the most brilliant as well as the most bitter and controversial of his satires. In each of its four books the hero, Lemuel Gulliver, embarks on a voyage, but shipwreck or some other hazard usually casts him up on a strange land. *Gulliver's Travels*'s matter-of-fact style and its air of sober reality confer on it an ironic depth that defeats oversimple explanations. Is it essentially comic, or is it a misanthropic depreciation of humankind? Pulling in different directions, this irony creates the tensions that are characteristic of Swift's best work, and reflects his vision of humanity's ambiguous position between bestiality and reasonableness.

Swift remained active throughout most of the 1730s—Dublin's foremost citizen and Ireland's great patriot dean. In the autumn of 1739 a great celebration was held in his honor. He had, however, begun to fail physically and later suffered a paralytic stroke, with subsequent aphasia. After his death in 1745, he was buried in St. Patrick's Cathedral.

VOLTAIRE

(b. Nov. 21, 1694, Paris, France—d. May 30, 1778, Paris)

Voltaire (the pseudonym of François-Marie Arouet) is one of the greatest of all French writers, known especially as a courageous crusader against tyranny, bigotry, and cruelty. He studied law but abandoned it to become a writer.

After the death of Louis XIV, in 1715, under the morally relaxed Regency, Voltaire became the wit of Parisian society, and his epigrams were widely quoted. In 1718, after the success of *Oedipe*, the first of his tragedies, he was acclaimed as the successor of the great classical dramatist Jean Racine and thenceforward adopted the name of Voltaire. (The origin of this pen name remains doubtful.) He continued to write for the theater all his life.

Voltaire was twice imprisoned in the Bastille for his remarks and in 1726 was exiled to England, where his philosophical interests deepened; he also learned English, and to the end of his life he was able to speak and write it fluently. He returned to France in 1728 or 1729. His epic poem *La Henriade* (1728) was well received, but his lampoons of the Regency and his liberal religious opinions caused offense. His *Lettres philosophiques* (1734) spoke out against established religious and political systems: they contrast the Empiricist psychology of the English philosopher John Locke with the conjectural lucubrations of the French philosopher René Descartes. A philosopher worthy of the name disdains empty, a priori speculations, Voltaire argues; he instead observes the facts and reasons from them.

The frankness of Voltaire's attack created an uproar. When a warrant of arrest was issued in 1734, he fled Paris and settled at Cirey in Champagne with Mme du Châtelet, who became his patroness and mistress. There he continued his theatrical writing, and he also turned to scientific research and the systematic study of religions and culture. Because of a lawsuit, he followed Mme du Châtelet to Brussels in May 1739, and thereafter they were constantly on the move between Belgium, Cirey, and Paris. After her death, in 1749, he spent periods in Berlin and Geneva; in

1754 he settled in Switzerland, and in 1758 he bought Ferney, a property on the Swiss border which, together with Tourney in France, enabled him, by crossing the frontier, to safeguard himself against police incursion from either country.

A period of intense and wide-ranging work followed, and there was scarcely a subject of importance on which he did not speak. In addition to his many works on philosophical and moral problems, he wrote *contes* ("tales"), including *Zadig* (1747), which is a kind of allegorical autobiography in which the Babylonian sage Zadig, like Voltaire, suffers persecution, is pursued by ill fortune, and ends by doubting the tender care of Providence for human beings, and *Micromégas* (1752), which measures the littleness of man in the cosmic scale. His best-known work, *Candide* (1759), is a satire on philosophical optimism. In it, the youth Candide, disciple of Doctor Pangloss (himself a disciple of the philosophical optimism of Leibniz), saw and suffered such misfortune that he was unable to believe that this was "the best of all possible worlds." Having retired with his companions to the shores of the Propontis, he discovered that the secret of happiness was "to cultivate one's garden," a practical philosophy excluding excessive idealism and nebulous metaphysics.

Voltaire's fame was now worldwide. As the "Innkeeper of Europe," as he was called, he welcomed such literary figures as James Boswell, Giovanni Casanova, Edward Gibbon, the Prince de Ligne, and the fashionable philosophers of Paris. He kept up an enormous correspondence—with the Philosophes, with his actresses and actors, and with those high in court circles, such as the duc de Richelieu (grandnephew of the Cardinal de Richelieu), the duc de Choiseul, and Mme du Barry, Louis XV's favorite. He renewed his correspondence with Frederick II and exchanged letters with Catherine II of

Russia. His main interest at this time, however, was his opposition to *l'infâme*, a word he used to designate the church, especially when it was identified with intolerance.

Voltaire's epic poetry, lyrical verse, and plays are virtually unknown today, but his *contes* are continually republished, and his letters are regarded as one of the great monuments of French literature. Yet it was the theater that brought Voltaire back to Paris in 1778. Wishing to direct the rehearsals of *Irène*, he made his triumphal return to the city he had not seen for 28 years. His health was profoundly impaired by the ensuing excitement, and he died several months later.

HENRY FIELDING

(b. April 22, 1707, Sharpham Park, Somerset, Eng.—d. Oct. 8, 1754, Lisbon, Port.)

Henry Fielding was a novelist and playwright who is considered one of the founders of the English novel. He began his literary career as a playwright who wrote satirical plays often targeting political corruption of the times. The passage in 1737 of the Licensing Act, by which all new plays had to be approved and licensed by the Lord Chamberlain before production, ended this work. Fielding then became a barrister but had little success. He probably wrote *Shamela* (1741), a burlesque of Samuel Richardson's novel *Pamela* that he never claimed.

Fielding's *Joseph Andrews* also satirizes *Pamela*, with Joseph, Pamela's virtuous footman brother, resisting the attempts of a highborn lady to seduce him. The parodic intention soon becomes secondary, and the novel develops into a masterpiece of sustained irony and social criticism. At its center is Parson Adams, one of the great comic figures of literature. Fielding explains in his preface that he is writing "a comic Epic-Poem in Prose." He was certainly inaugurating a new genre in fiction.

Journalistic work after the Jacobite Rebellion of 1745 made Fielding a trusted supporter of the government. His reward came in 1748, when he was appointed justice of the peace (or magistrate) for Westminster and Middlesex, with his own courthouse, which was also his residence, in Bow Street in central London. Together with his blind half brother, John Fielding, also a magistrate, he turned an office without honor—it carried no salary—into one of great dignity and importance and established a new tradition of justice and the suppression of crime in London. Among other things, Fielding strengthened the police force at his disposal by recruiting a small body of able and energetic "thieftakers"—the Bow Street Runners.

The History of Tom Jones, a Foundling (1749), with its great comic gusto, vast gallery of characters, and contrasted scenes of high and low life in London and the provinces, has always constituted the most popular of his works. Like its predecessor, *Joseph Andrews*, it is constructed around a romance plot. The hero, whose true identity remains unknown until the denouement, loves the beautiful Sophia Western, and at the end of the book he wins her hand. Numerous obstacles have to be overcome before he achieves this, however, and in the course of the action the various sets of characters pursue each other from one part of the country to another, giving Fielding an opportunity to paint an incomparably vivid picture of England in the mid-18th century. The introductory chapters at the beginning of each book make it clear how carefully Fielding had considered the problem of planning the novel. No novelist up until then had so clear an idea of what a novel should be, so that it is not surprising that *Tom Jones* is a masterpiece of literary engineering.

Amelia (1751), a much more somber work, anticipates the Victorian domestic novel, being a study of the relationship between a man and his wife. It is also Fielding's most intransigent representation of the evils of the society in which he lived, and he clearly finds the spectacle no longer comic.

SAMUEL JOHNSON

(b. Sept. 18, 1709, Lichfield, Staffordshire, Eng.—d. Dec. 13, 1784, London)

Samuel Johnson, an English critic, biographer, essayist, poet, and lexicographer, is regarded as one of the greatest figures of 18th-century life and letters.

Johnson was the son of a poor bookseller. In 1728 he entered Pembroke College, Oxford. He stayed only 13 months, until December 1729, because he lacked the funds to continue. Johnson then became undermaster at Market Bosworth grammar school in 1732 but was unhappy there; with only £20 inheritance from his father, he left his position with the feeling that he was escaping prison. In 1735 Johnson married Elizabeth Porter, a widow 20 years his senior. His wife's marriage settlement enabled him to open a school in Edial, near Lichfield, the following year. One of his students, David Garrick, would become the greatest English actor of the age and a lifelong friend, though their friendship was not without its strains. The school soon proved a failure, however, and he and Garrick left for London in 1737.

A year later Johnson began his long association with *The Gentleman's Magazine*, often considered the first modern magazine, with a wide range of poetry and prose. In the mid-1740s he began to work toward two of his major literary accomplishments. His *Miscellaneous Observations on the Tragedy of Macbeth* (1745), intended as a preliminary sample of his work, was his first significant Shakespeare criticism, which remains his greatest work of literary criticism. The work culminated in his editing an edition of Shakespeare, which appeared in eight volumes in 1765. Johnson edited and annotated the text and wrote a preface.

In 1746 he wrote *The Plan of a Dictionary of the English Language* and signed a contract for *A Dictionary of the English Language*, which was eventually published in two volumes in 1755—six years later than planned, but remarkably quickly for so extensive an undertaking. There had been earlier English dictionaries, but none on the scale of Johnson's. In addition to giving etymologies, not the strong point of Johnson and his contemporaries, and definitions, in which he excelled, Johnson illustrated usage with quotations drawn almost entirely from writing from the Elizabethan period to his own time.

Johnson's other works include *The Vanity of Human Wishes* (1749), his most impressive poem as well as the first work published with his name, and the long fiction *Rasselas* (originally published as *The Prince of Abissinia: A Tale*), which he wrote in 1759, during the evenings of a single week, in order to be able to pay for the funeral of his mother. His many essays appeared in the periodicals *The Rambler* (1750–52), *The Literary Magazine* (from 1756), and *The Universal Chronicle* (in a series known as *The Idler*, 1758–60), among others.

In 1765 Johnson received an honorary Doctor of Laws degree from Trinity College, Dublin, and 10 years later he was awarded the Doctor of Civil Laws from the University of Oxford. He never referred to himself as Dr. Johnson, though a number of his contemporaries did; James Boswell's consistent use of the title in his famous biography of Johnson, *The Life of Samuel Johnson, LL.D.* (1791), made it popular.

In the early 1770s Johnson wrote a series of political pamphlets supporting positions favorable to the government but in keeping with his own views. His subsequent works include *A Journey to the Western Islands of Scotland* (1775), based on travels with Boswell, and *Prefaces, Biographical and Critical, to the Works of the English Poets* (conventionally known as *The Lives of the Poets*), which was conceived modestly as short prefatory notices to an edition of English poetry but which expanded in scope so that Johnson's prefaces alone filled the first 10 volumes (1779–81) and the poetry grew to 56 volumes.

While Johnson is well remembered for his aphorisms—which contributed to his becoming, after Shakespeare, the most frequently quoted of English writers—his criticism is, perhaps, the most significant part of his writings. Through his *Dictionary*, his edition of Shakespeare, and his *Lives of the Poets* in particular, he helped invent what we now call "English Literature."

JOHANN WOLFGANG VON GOETHE

(b. Aug. 28, 1749, Frankfurt am Main [Germany]—d. March 22, 1832, Weimar, Saxe-Weimar)

Johann Wolfgang von Goethe was a poet, playwright, novelist, scientist, statesman, theater director, critic, and amateur artist. He is considered the greatest German literary figure of the modern era.

Goethe is the only German literary figure whose range and international standing equal those of Germany's supreme philosophers (who have often drawn on his works and ideas) and composers (who have often set his works to music). In the literary culture of the German-speaking countries, he has had so dominant a position that, since the end of the 18th century, his writings have been described as "classical." In a European perspective he appears as the central and unsurpassed representative of the Romantic movement, broadly understood. He could be said to stand in the same relation to the culture of the era that began with the Enlightenment and continues to the present day as William Shakespeare does to the culture of the Renaissance and Dante to the culture of the High Middle Ages. His *Faust*, though eminently stage-worthy when suitably edited, is also Europe's greatest long poem since John Milton's *Paradise Lost*, if not since Dante's *The Divine Comedy*.

Early Works

From April 1770 until August 1771 Goethe studied in Strasbourg for the doctorate. However, he had now emerged from his Christian period, and for his dissertation he chose a potentially shocking subject from ecclesiastical law concerning the nature of ancient Jewish religion. The dissertation, which questioned the status of the Ten Commandments, proved too scandalous to be accepted, as perhaps he intended, and he took instead the Latin oral examination for the licentiate in law (which by convention also conferred the title of doctor).

He later returned to Frankfurt. There he created a first draft over six weeks in the autumn of 1771 of *Geschichte Gottfriedens von Berlichingen mit der eisernen Hand, dramatisirt* ("The History of Gottfried von Berlichingen with the Iron Hand, Dramatized"), later titled simply *Götz von Berlichingen*. It was eventually translated by Sir Walter Scott, who was inspired by Goethe's example to think of using his own local history as the material for his novels. It also contains, however, an invented love-intrigue, focusing on the weak-willed Weislingen, a man who is unable to remain faithful to a worthy woman and betrays his class origins for the sake of a brilliant career. *Götz* was not published immediately but became known to a few friends in manuscript, and Goethe, already well-connected at the cultivated local court of Darmstadt, was asked to start reviewing for a new intellectual Frankfurt journal, the *Frankfurter Gelehrte Anzeigen* ("Frankfurt Review of Books"), which was hostile to the enlightened despotism of the German princely states, notably Prussia and Austria. He thereby effectively became part of the literary movement subsequently known as the Sturm und Drang ("Storm and Stress").

The years from 1773 to 1776 proved to be the most productive period in Goethe's life; poems and other works, mainly fragments, poured out. *Die Leiden des jungen Werthers* (*The Sorrows of Young Werther*), written in two months early in 1774, appeared that autumn and captured the imagination of a generation. It was almost immediately translated into French and in 1779 into English. The uncompromising concentration on the principal character's viewpoint—no one else's letters are communicated to the reader—permits the depiction from within of emotional and intellectual disintegration and partly accounts for the strength of the public reaction. Much moral outrage was generated by a work that appeared to condone both adultery and suicide, but for 35 years Goethe was known in the first instance as the author of *Werther*.

A Change in Perspective

In 1775, after an invitation to visit the court of the young new duke of Weimar, Goethe arrived at Weimar, where he accepted an appointment to the ducal court; he would remain there, on the whole, for the rest of his life. His presence helped to establish Weimar as a literary and intellectual center. But Goethe was never entirely at ease in his role of Weimar courtier and official, and his literary output suffered. Until 1780, he continued to produce original and substantial works—particularly, in 1779, a prose drama, *Iphigenie auf Tauris* (*Iphigenia in Tauris*). Thereafter, however, he found it increasingly difficult to complete anything, and the flow of poetry, which had been getting thinner, all but dried up. He kept himself going as a writer by forcing himself to write one book of a novel, *Wilhelm Meisters theatralische Sendung* (*The Theatrical Mission of Wilhelm Meister*), each year until 1785. In a rough-and-tumble, ironic way, reminiscent of the English novelist Henry Fielding, the novel tells the story of a gifted young man who aims for stardom in a reformed German national theatrical culture. At first the plot was transparently autobiographical, but Goethe's own development gradually diverged from that of his hero, and the novel remained in manuscript during his lifetime. For 10 years Goethe turned away completely from publishing; the last lengthy work of his to be printed before the silence was *Stella* in 1776.

Goethe spent most of the years from 1786 to 1788 in Italy, away from the court and its pressures and disappointments. As a geologist, he climbed Vesuvius; as a connoisseur of ancient art, he visited Pompeii and Herculaneum. He consulted others about his own drawing and joined the circle of the British ambassador in Naples, Sir William Hamilton, and the actress who was later to be, as Emma, Lady Hamilton, the ambassador's wife and Lord Nelson's mistress. In Sicily he had reached a landscape impregnated with a Greek past, in which Homer's *Odyssey* seemed not fanciful but realistic; later he even toyed with the idea that Homer might have been a Sicilian. What Goethe came to value most about this time was not the opportunity of seeing ancient and Renaissance works of art and architecture firsthand but rather the opportunity of living as nearly as possible what he thought of as the ancient way of life, experiencing the benign climate and fertile setting in which human beings and nature were in harmony. His return to Weimar in June 1788 was extremely reluctant.

New Ventures

By his 40th birthday, in 1789, Goethe had all but completed the collected edition of his works, but he seems not to have known where to go next as a poet. A drama failed; he tinkered with satires and translations. Perhaps by way of compensation, he turned to science. In 1790 he published his theory of the principles of botany, *Versuch, die Metamorphose der Pflanzen zu erklären* ("Essay in Elucidation of the Metamorphosis of Plants"; English translation in *Goethe's Botany*), an attempt to show that all plant forms are determined by a process of alternating expansion and contraction of a basic unit, the leaf. In 1791, however, a completely new scientific issue began to obsess him: the theory of color. Convinced that Newton was wrong to assume that white light could be broken into light of different colors, Goethe proposed a new approach of his own.

In 1794 the poet and dramatist Friedrich Schiller suggested that he and Goethe should collaborate on a new journal, *Die Horen* (*The Horae*), intended to give literature a voice in an age increasingly dominated by politics. The friendship with Schiller began a new period in Goethe's life, in some ways one of the happiest and, from a literary point of view, one of the most productive. In *The Horae* he published a collection of short stories, *Unterhaltungen deutscher Ausgewanderten* ("Conversations of German Émigrés"; Eng. trans. *The German Refugees*), which were found tedious, and the *Roman Elegies*, which were found scandalous, and serialized a translation of the autobiography of Florentine Mannerist artist Benvenuto Cellini, which was acceptable but unexciting.

Schiller soon lost interest in the journal, which ceased publication after three years. Perhaps it had served its purpose simply by initiating the collaboration with Goethe, which was closer, longer, and on a higher level than any comparable friendship in world literature. The poets began a correspondence, which ran to over a thousand letters, and for over 10 years they discussed each other's works and projects, as well as those of their contemporaries, in conversation and writing. Both profited incalculably from the relationship. But in early 1805 Schiller and Goethe both fell seriously ill. Schiller died. Goethe recovered but felt that, with Schiller dead, he had lost "the half of my existence."

In 1806 Napoleon routed the Prussian armies at the Battle of Jena. Weimar, 12 miles from the battle, was subsequently occupied and sacked, though Goethe's house was spared, thanks to Napoleon's admiration for the author of *Werther*. In 1808 he met Napoleon during the Congress of Erfurt and was made a knight of the Legion of Honor. He became reconciled to Napoleon's rule, regarding it as a more or less legitimate successor to the Holy Roman Empire, and, in the relatively peaceful interval after the Austrian war against France in 1809, a new serenity entered his writing. But that ended during the years 1814–17, after the overthrow of Napoleon's dominion by allied troops at the Battle of Leipzig (1813). Alienation from the modern age is the undertone in all his work of this period.

Later Years

In his final years he experienced a time of extraordinary, indeed probably unparalleled literary achievement by a man of advanced age. He prepared a final collected edition of his works, initially in 40 volumes, the *Ausgabe letzter Hand* ("Edition of the Last Hand"). He wrote a fourth section of his autobiography, completing the story of his life up to his departure for Weimar in 1775; he compiled an account of his time in Rome in 1787–88, *Zweiter Römischer*

Aufenthalt (1829; "Second Sojourn in Rome"); and above all he wrote part two of *Faust*, of which only a few passages had been drafted in 1800.

Work on *Faust* accompanied Goethe throughout his adult life. Of a possible plan in 1769 to dramatize the story of the man who sold his soul to the Devil in exchange for earthly fulfillment, perhaps including his ultimate redemption, no firm evidence survives. The first published version, *Faust: ein Fragment*, appeared in 1790, with *Faust: Part One* following in 1808 and *Faust: Part Two* in 1832. *Part Two* is, in a sense, a poetic reckoning with Goethe's own times, with their irresistible dynamism and their alienation from his Classical ideal of fulfilled humanity. As with much of Goethe's later work, its richness, complexity, and literary daring began to be appreciated only in the 20th century.

The year 1829 brought celebrations throughout Germany of Goethe's 80th birthday. In the spring of 1832, having caught a cold, he died of a heart attack.

ROBERT BURNS

(b. Jan. 25, 1759, Alloway, Ayrshire, Scot.—d. July 21, 1796, Dumfries, Dumfriesshire)

Robert Burns, considered the national poet of Scotland, wrote lyrics and songs in the Scottish dialect of English. He was also famous for his amours and his rebellion against orthodox religion and morality.

Watching his father die a worn-out and bankrupt man in 1784 helped to make Burns both a rebel against the social order of his day and a bitter satirist of all forms of religious and political thought that condoned or perpetuated inhumanity. He received some formal schooling from a teacher as well as sporadically from other sources. He acquired a superficial reading knowledge of French and a bare smattering of Latin, and he read most of the important 18th-century English writers as well as Shakespeare, Milton, and Dryden. His knowledge of Scottish literature was confined in his childhood to orally transmitted folk songs and folk tales together with a modernization of the late 15th-century poem *Wallace*.

Proud, restless, and full of a nameless ambition, the young Burns did his share of hard work on his family's farm. He developed rapidly throughout 1784 and 1785 as an "occasional" poet who more and more turned to verse to express his emotions of love, friendship, or amusement or his ironical contemplation of the social scene. But these were not spontaneous effusions by an almost-illiterate peasant. Burns was a conscious craftsman; his entries in the commonplace book that he had begun in 1783 reveal that from the beginning he was interested in the technical problems of versification. Though he wrote poetry for his own amusement and that of his friends, Burns remained dissatisfied. In the midst of personal and economic troubles he published *Poems, Chiefly in the Scottish Dialect* in 1786. Its success with simple country folk and sophisticated Edinburgh critics alike was immediate and overwhelming. It included a handful of first-rate Scots poems: *The Twa Dogs*, *Scotch Drink*, *The Holy Fair*, *An Address to the Deil*, *The Death and Dying Words of Poor Maillie*, *To a Mouse*, *To a Louse*, and some others, including a number of verse letters addressed to various friends. In addition, there were six gloomy and histrionic poems in English, four songs, of which only one, "It Was Upon a Lammas Night," showed promise of his future greatness as a song writer.

Burns moved to Edinburgh in 1786 and was lionized, patronized, and showered with well-meant but dangerous advice. After a number of amorous and other adventures there and several trips to other parts of Scotland, he settled in the summer of 1788 at a farm in Ellisland, Dumfriesshire. At Edinburgh, too, he arranged for a new and enlarged edition (1787) of his *Poems*.

In Edinburgh Burns had met James Johnson, a keen collector of Scottish songs who was bringing out a series of volumes of songs with the music and who enlisted Burns's help in finding, editing, improving, and rewriting items. Burns was enthusiastic and soon became virtual editor of Johnson's *The Scots Musical Museum*. Later, he became involved with a similar project for George Thomson, but Thomson was a more consciously genteel person than Johnson, and Burns had to fight with him to prevent him from "refining" words and music and so ruining their character. Johnson's *The Scots Musical Museum* (1787–1803) and the first five volumes of Thomson's *A Select Collection of Original Scotish Airs for the Voice* (1793–1818) contain the bulk of Burns's songs. Burns spent the latter part of his life in assiduously collecting and writing songs to provide words for traditional Scottish airs. He obtained a post in the excise service in 1789 and moved to Dumfries in 1791, where he lived until his death. He wrote numerous "occasional" poems and did an immense amount of work for the two song collections.

It is by his songs that Burns is best known, and it is his songs that have carried his reputation around the world. Burns is without doubt the greatest songwriter Great Britain has produced. He wrote all his songs to known tunes, sometimes writing several sets of words to the same air. Many songs which must have been written by Burns he never claimed as his. He never claimed "Auld Lang Syne," for example, which he described simply as an old fragment he had discovered, but the song we have is almost certainly his, though the chorus and probably the first stanza are old. (Burns wrote it for a simple and moving old air that is *not* the tune to which it is now sung, as Thomson set it to another tune.) The full extent of Burns's work on Scottish song will probably never be known.

Glossary

allegory: The use of fictional figures and actions to symbolize truths or generalizations about human existence.

aphorism: A short phrase that expresses a truth.

apologist: A person who defends a group, cause, or idea that's under attack.

burlesque: A literary work that presents a serious subject in a comical way.

conceit: A theme or concept.

dramatist: Someone who writes plays.

epic poem: Long and highly stylized poetry that details the heroic achievements of the main protagonist.

lampoon: To publicly make fun of or criticize someone or something in a comical way.

novellas: Short narratives with their origins in medieval Italy.

picaresque: Describes a story that involves a rogue or adventurer surviving mainly by his or her wits in a treacherous society.

prose: Writing that is not poetry.

sabi: Love of the old, the faded, and the unobtrusive.

satire: Something that makes fun of and shows the weaknesses of human nature.

verisimilitude: The quality of seeming real or true.

vicissitude: A sudden or unexpected change in one's life; the ability of life to change quickly and without warning.

For More Information

BOOKS

Defoe, Daniel. *The Life and Adventures of Robinson Crusoe.* San Tan, AZ: Pure Snow Publishing, 2021.

Johnson, Samuel. *Samuel Johnson: Selected Works.* New Haven, CT: Yale University Press, 2021.

Ng, Freeman. *Basho's Haiku Journeys*. Berkeley, CA: Stone Bridge Press, 2021.

Swift, Jonathan. *Gulliver's Travels: Into Several Remote Nations of the World.* Orinda, CA: SeaWolf Press, 2022.

WEBSITES

All Poetry

allpoetry.com/Matsuo-Basho

Read about the life of Bashō and listen to or read some of his most famous haikus.

Folger Shakespeare Library

www.folger.edu/

Learn more about William Shakespeare through the Folger Shakespeare Library, which has the world's largest Shakespeare collection.

Poetry Foundation

www.poetryfoundation.org/poets/john-donne

This site offers biographical information about John Donne and a selection of his poetry.

Poets.org

poets.org/poem/you-foolish-men

Read an English translation of "You Foolish Men," a poem by Sor Juana Inés de la Cruz.

Index